The
Village
Princess

Based on True Events

Rampria Mohana Sundaram

Co-author:
Bhavithra Mohana Sundaram

PARTRIDGE

Co-author: Bhavithra Mohana Sundaram

ISBN:	Softcover	978-1-5437-4423-1
	eBook	978-1-5437-4424-8

Print information available on the last page.

To order additional copies of this book, contact
Toll Free 800 101 2657 (Singapore)
Toll Free 1 800 81 7340 (Malaysia)
orders.singapore@partridgepublishing.com

www.partridgepublishing.com/singapore

Dedication

My all time gratitude to the most loveable lady in this world, my iron lady, my mother, Uma Chadayandy for being very supportive and let me to complete my dreams without any restrictions. Followed by that, infinite love and thank you to my super duper talented and amazing girl, Bhavitha Mohana Sundaram for playing big part in making every single part of this book. My co-author, idea maker, motivation buster, co-sponsor, magic creator, lucky star and my sister, thanks for giving me a opportunity for me to create a historical combination with you, **The BhaRia's**.

Millions of thanks to everyone who supported me all the way in making this book which is a dream came true moment especially the three most important people in my life as well as for the development for this book, Lavanya Valayutham and Livenraj Rajendran (The L&L) along with my buddy Rajmohan Sivalingam for being with me from nothing till everything. Thanks for keep on motivating me, advising and criticizing at each and every step that I took for this book. Love you guys in tones.

Thanks to all my friends, my friends family members and everyone that I had missed from the list. Last but not least, lots of love and thanks to Shamala Chadayandy, the sole reason for this book to be published. The great soul who had inspired me with her stories since I was a kid. So, this book is truly dedicated to you '*perima*' and all the lovely people that you met throughout your beautiful journey including Madam Betty, Banso sir, Gian Franco sir, Marco sir, Bravislla sir, and others that I missed to mention here.

∞love from The BhaRia's

1

Breathing.

Shamala did not felt alive being there. Like anything would ever be normal again, after leaving the one who really loved her and sitting in *Metropolitan* (Rome metro), like nothing had happened in her life. The train was speeding just like her thoughts.

'Prossima fermata, Re Di Roma'. (Next destination, Rome)

The announcement interrupted her train of thoughts. Shamala get off and as usual her feet strolled to her favorite spot of the town.

"Miss, here you go," leaving a cup of coffee in front of Shamala, the waiter bowed with full of respect and went away leaving her alone.

Red...Why? Why are you torturing me?

Shamala mumbled trying to forget the bitter scenes which take up residence in her mind. Staring at the red cup for a couple of minutes and her brain start to race again. The two magnificent words, turns out to be ordeal. Perhaps, there is no such thing as 'Lucky Life'. Again and again, the colour of the cup forcefully dragged Shamala to remember the incident that could be avoided, the incident which takes her happiness away, and the incident where her fiancée was lying on a pool of blood.

"*Oh mio piccolo principe!*" (Oh my charming little prince!) admired Maria Theresa seeing her youngest son in the best outfit of the town. "*Dov'è la tua bellezza mia cara? A che ora arriverà qui?*" (Where is your beauty my dear? What time she will reach here?)

"My princess will arrive soon *mamma* (mother). The car that was sent to pick up her broke down halfway but don't worry, I've sent another car and you knew how my buddy flies on the road," Danielle patting his beloved mother with convincing laughter left Maria Theresa not to worry about Shamala.

The Place of De Bulla lit with enormous gleaming chandeliers, decorating the place with compelling light rays and a majestic fountain with two gigantic bulls in the middle, with pieces of mirrors reflecting the light rays and soothing flow of water could be heard each and every corner. Adding to the grand occasion, a long table was set and the aroma from the scrumptious food prepared by the best chefs' of the town, instigating the taste buds of each and everyone to devour.

"*Lei è quella?*" (She's the one?)

"*Gesù, è incantevole!*" (Jesus, she's enchanting!)

"*Una ragazza così bella!*" (Such a beautiful girl!)

Whispers of praises admiring the beauty of the most awaited lady of the day filled every nook of the palace. Shamala wearing a long cream coloured gown, walking gracefully, sided by Betty and Banso, heading towards Danielle and his family. The celebration of the sensational event begins. Grand music from drums, trumpets and violin accompanied with songs from the choir singing in high note welcomes the demurely looking lady and her family. Danielle with full pride ambled few steps towards his lady and bow in order to hold her hand. There was a soft light in her eyes, as she gave her hand to Danielle.

"I could not take my eyes off you *bella* (beautiful)," Danielle expressing his amazement of Shamala's beauty. "Not forgetting your million dollars smile too. I wonder how you could do that. Love you a lot *bella*."

Warm air filled with loving words flowing into Shamala's ear, hitting her eardrums. She could not react. She could not move. As if her legs were rooted to the marble floor. Everything is too sudden, unusual, uncommon and odd for a 28-year old Indian girl from abroad.

Maria Theresa starts the engagement with a small speech representing 'The Bulla's' and Betty from the bride side. And the most awaited part of the party was completed when Daniella and Shamala exchange their beautifully initial crafted engagement ring in presence of hundreds of people. Happiness is on the air and celebration continues till midnight.

2

New environment. New place. New people. Once again, life blooms for Shamala, returning from her ordeal-experienced, hardened and bitter. Her journey in finding the purpose of her life which starts at *Re Di Roma,* taught her endless life lesson and now it's continuing at *Basilica S. Paula*

"*Bambola* (Doll) did Marco inform you that he gonna bring you out for dinner tonight? You better go with him my dear, or else I don't know which girl he will bring today," wondered Roberta.

"Tonight?"

"Yes. Pass me the watering can *bambola,*" added Roberta. "Do you want to go somewhere else tonight?"

"No, but how can I leave you all alone?" worried Shamala.

"Hahahaha. Stop worrying about me. I'm not that old," simpered the 85 year old Roberta while watering her flower pots.

'Roberta and Marco', the new pillar of hope for Shamala in searching for her life purpose. Deteriorating health condition of Roberta, forced her only son Marco to find for a helper. And that is how, Shamala ended as an assistant for Roberta. Both mother and son seem to be wealthy, but kindness and care that they showered on Shamala are invaluable.

"Madam, it's time for you to take the medicine," reminded Shamala.

"Oh no, not again!" shrieked Roberta.

"You have too," chuckled Shamala peeping at Roberta's unpleasant reaction.

Ding Dong!

"I'll get the door", Shamala trotted to entrance

"*Hola* (hello) *bambola, hola mamma,*" greeted Marco while handing his briefcase to Shamala.

"What a surprise my son," smiled Roberta. "Coming back home early in the evening."

Marco laughed. "*Mamma*, is that a form of sarcasm? I just want to spend more time with the queen of my heart." Marco clasped Roberta in his arm. He assures that nobody could take his mother's place in his heart. Only he knew how the iron lady raised him as a single mother and now he had touch the peak of wealth but this wouldn't have happened if Roberta had gave up on their life when hard time strikes.

Standing still at the corner of Marco's study room, Shamala was admiring Marco and Roberta expressing their mother-son love.

I miss my family too.

Leaning her head on the back of the wall, Shamala reflected her childhood moments. Those time that she spent together with her *appa* (father) at the paddy field, outing with her elder brother to town and getting chided by *amma (mother)* for coming back late after 'Marble Tournament' with buddies. Warm tears rolled on her cheeks.

"*Bambola*, are you okay?"

Lost in her thoughts, Shamala didn't even notice that Marco had stepped into the room. Wiping her tears off, Shamala tried to hide her sadness with her smile.

"Is something wrong? Are you okay?"

"I'm okay Marco. No worries," Shamala assured to avoid being questioned by Marco.

"But your eyes don't show that you are okay," Marco opined.

"No. Believe me," Shamala trying to convince Marco. "What time are we going out? Are your colleagues joining us?"

"Emmm… Around eight and only two of us".

"It's rainy out there. Shall we eat pizza?" Marco gave a look at Shamala who was sitting beside, drowned deep in her world.

Is she really okay? Is something bothering her?

Marco's brain clouded with questions seeing Shamala's gloomy state. He still remembers his first meeting with Shamala, when he and Roberta went to pick her up at the *Metropolitan*. They were marveled to see a small, thin lady with long nice hair, wearing a decent jumper walking towards them with a lovely smile on her face.

They said she is thirty but she looks like fifteen.

Marco trying to recollect his conversation with Banso, Shamala's former employer.

Teeeeeeeettt… Marco's Ferrari screeched to a halt behind honking at the reckless driver.

"Be careful," Shamala exclaimed vehemently

"Thank god, finally someone is back from Wonderland," mumbled Marco giving a warm look to Shamala. The car stopped. Marco parked the car and both of them walk to a pizza stall.

"Two pizza please," ordered Marco. "Cappuccino for you Bambola?"

"No, just a cup of coffee please. Shall we sit Marco?" Shamala glumly asked

"Yes," he hummed, grabbing two cups of hot black coffee.

Marco followed Shamala's heavy steps, walking towards a bench.

"*Bambola* enough. This is more than enough. What happened? Please do feel comfortable to share with me," Marco trying to free his knots of curiosity. "Shamala, everyone thinks that you and I are having something in between. You know … something like more than a friend," Marco spluttered.

Looking at the white smoky steam with irresistible aroma escaping in the air and vanishing in blink of eyes, Shamala was sitting quietly, musing over Marco's word.

"But, only you and I knew, what is going on between us. The way that you took care of me, the affection that you showed, you knew how lucky I felt after you came in my life, taking away my loneliness and filling the space of happiness. Not everyone could do this. But you did my dear. Since the day you stepped into the house, I've got a sister to chat and after *mamma*, you are my place to seek comfort. And I still remember that you used to say that, with my presence you could overcome your sadness of not seeing your little brother. But now something is bothering my dearest, but she is not allowing her little brother to help her. Isn't that sad to hear?" questioned Marco in forlorn.

"I'm sorry Marco. I didn't mean to do that but I just don't want to bother you," explained Shamala.

"How could you think of me like that? Don't I have the rights to share your sorrows?" Marco questioned.

"Of course you do Marco. Thank you… Thank you so much for the care that you have on me." Contemplating on how to start and where to start, Shamala's mind went for a roller coaster ride recalling her memories.

3

"Ah Meng!" yelled Shamala. "Wait for me at the orchard, *amma* (mother) asked me to wash the pots. I'll meet you there once I've finished. Okay?"

"Aiyaah... Ok...OK... I wait for you," taking a glimpse at Shamala's house, Ah Meng went towards the orchard.

It was a small village at Teluk Intan, Malaysia. There was a reputable family, very well known for their nature of helping people in need. Paddy field, maize plantation, fruit orchard, hens, cows, goats, birds and a small house surrounded by *rambutan* trees filled with 12 members. People used to envy on them but only Chadyan and Kalyan know how much they had gone through to make till the end. Besides the blessed life, they were known compared to other villagers due to their children beautiful outer appearance.

The father to four handsome boys and six lovely girls, Chadyan was eight feet tall, with dark brown eyes and almond coloured skin, he was once the most handsome boy, hard-working, intelligent and eligible bachelor who eventually got married to the village head daughter, Kalyan. She is the major reason on why their children look eye-catchy. Blessed with fair complexion, light-brown cat eyes and demure looking Kalyan had been the dream of the village.

To all the might, all the children can be said to be blessed with their parent's remarkable genes. But, out of ten, nine of them were praised by villagers except for one skinny little girl with dark-coloured skin caused by her adventure in finding for happiness with her friends under glazing sun and the shortest among the six daughters, and her name is Shamala or more likely to be known as Mala. Having all the dominant traits, young Mala never cared about harsh words commenting on her appearance.

For Shamala, that entire she cared about was her friends. Friends for life. Friends that always accompanies her to make life more happening and awesome. Ah Meng, Asan, Nina and Mala made the whole village going nuts. As per the villagers, kids were labeled good if they stay at home, obeying parents instruction and obtain good mark in exams. These 'criteria' of good kids eventually leads irritation and hatred towards the four kids who enjoyed their childhood in their own way. Roaming around the village, Shamala and her 'gang' were innovative kids who used their creativity to invent games using scraps, leaves, woods and whichever things that have potential to be turned into something to play with.

"Malaaaaa……" bawled Kalyan seeing a pile of unwashed dishes stacked near the wall.

What I'm going to do with this lucky girl.

"School again!" Shamala perplexed. "No I'm not interested *appa* (father). It's not getting into my brain. Then what do you expect me to do?" argued Shamala.

"Why? What's the problem? Ram and Muniamma can complete their SRP. Chamundeshwari and Kanna are top scorers in school, but you? What is your problem Mala," queried her mother as sign of dissatisfaction on Shamala's adamancy for not continuing her studies.

"But *amma*, Chinna *anna* (elder brother) had stopped after Standard 3. You were okay with that. Why? Because he helps our family to find source of money and why am I not allowed to do that? I want to help my family too. You always said that we had lots of money in past but now, only 'Good Family' tittle left. I heard enough *amma*. After I was born, our family faced a lot of troubles and eventually we strive for food. Poverty hits us so bad and now you are not letting me to help. Why *amma*? Am I that unlucky? Am I such a bad omen? I may look ugly but it doesn't mean that I cannot do anything for the family," Shamala sobbing at the window edge.

"Okay, okay, you can work but before that stop crying," Chadyan acquiesced. "You want to follow *appa* for work right? *Appa* don't mind. But remember, you Shouldn't regret in your future."

Shamala's wish to help her family had been approved by the head of the family. Instead of doing similar chores such as cooking, cleaning, knitting, sewing and decorating, she enjoyed her teenage period at oil palm plantation, farms and climbing coconut tree was her favourite. Shamala loves her lifestyle and the way her father treats her. She grew up to be courageous and optimistic. While other girls are busy decorating themselves with ribbons, *saree* (Indian traditional wear for woman), dress and skirts, Shamala rocks the village with her cowboy attire. She leads her life in her own style — cool.

"Bye Ah Meng. It's time for 'Little House on the Prairie'. I need to go," rushed Shamala leaving Ah Meng under the tree with marbles on the ground.

"Oikkk, this is not fair. You cannot leave the game halfway. This is cheating", chided Ah Meng in hope to stop her.

"I can stay, I wanted to stay but I'll go crazy if I miss the episode," Shamala vacillated.

"Do I care?" Ah Meng spat. "Unless you tell me something about your Little House story."

"Emmm… Okay but promise that you will buy a bowl of curry mi. Deal?" grinned Shamala in spite of the fact that Ah Meng never fulfills his promise.

"A bowl? It costs five cents". Ah Meng showing his pity face to his friend. "Where will I get the money?"

"Do I care?" Shamala cackled.

"*Aiyaaaah*... Ok *lah*! Ok *lah*! Tell me the story," Ah Meng trying to stop his friend who is laughing in a shrill.

"This story is similar to Cinderella but it has something more," Shamala starting the story.

"Who is Cinderella?" Ah Meng questioned in curiosity.

Shamala gave a sharp look to Ah Meng.

This gonna be difficult for me.

"Emmmmmm... Cinderella is a story about a poor girl, tortured by her stepmother and stepsister. But due to her good heart, in the end she got married to a prince," Shamala trying to make Ah Meng remember about the classic story.

"Oooooooo... that girl, but didn't she die because she ate the poisoned apple." Ah Meng questioned.

Shamala's face started to turn sour. "*Arghhhhh* Ah Meng, that's Snow White!"

"Hahahahaha. I told you I don't know who Cinderella is."

4

From small village, Perak to big town, Penang, Shamala does not have enough education to join work as professional doctor or teacher at that time but strong-willed Shamala did not lose hope. She understands that she needs to start from bottom.

"Today 'Big Boss' will be coming to factory. So, I need to go early. Finish up the house chores and I'll see you at the factory," instructed her sister Angalaparameshwari.

There will be always love when two hearts are far but once it is near, hatred will come instantly. Time change, people change and the sad part is my sister had changed.

Shamala remembered these lines of her favourite song which she relates to her current life.

Joining as an ordinary operator in a factory where her elder sister was working as 'Line Leader'. Everything seems to be nice at first as Angalaparameshwari treats her sister well. Cooking delicious food, cracking jokes and eating together will be their daily routine. Every day, Shamala follows her sister to workplace by car but nothing stays stagnant. Cooking stops, jokes stops, eating together stops and no more car pleasure for Shamala. Walking and public transportation becomes Shamala's best friend. To displace anger on Shamala, plates and cups becomes victims. Shamala endured all, but God never let good people to suffer for a long period of time.

"How are you Nina? I didn't expect this call from you," Shamala being thankful to her childhood friend who calls to wish birthday to Shamala. "So how's your life Nina? Working or planning to get married?"

"It's not that easy for people to accept dark-skinned girl as bride these days Shamala," lamented Nina remembering the family who rejected her marriage proposal. "I've decided to go for work at Kuala Lumpur (KL). High pay, good work. Life settled. No need to depend on anyone. Isn't that great Shamala?"

"Are you sure? You want to go to KL? You got job there?" Shamala shoots unstoppable questions.

"Mala it's just KL. Not America my dear," Nina trying to calm down her friends brain. "I'll be staying with a European family. They need a helper as they are very busy with her business, they want someone to do housekeeping at their house. Siva *anne* (elder brother Siva) is the one who told me about this work.

Helper. Staying with a family. Something new. Shamala thinking on the her friend's words.

"Hello? Mala? Are you still on the line?"

"Ah.... Yes... Yes... Sorry was thinking about something. Nina. If you don't mind can you find this kind of job for me? I want to leave this house. Please help me," requested Shamala.

"You want to leave your current job?"

"Yes. Don't ask me why. But I need to move to a new environment," Shamala articulated.

"Okay. I won't ask and yeah, I remember something. There is an Italian family who needs helper too. Would you like to work there?"

"Italian family?" thought Shamala.

It had been one work, Shamala staying at Damansara, Kuala Lumpur with Betty and Banso, a lovely Italian and Brazilian mixed couple. Still in shock, but everytime when Shamala stumbled to communicate with them, her employers were always ready to guide her. Shamala introduced herself to her new employee with words taught by Nina

"I finished cleaning madam. Any other work? Shall I cook?" asked Shamala.

"Today, you don't need to cook young lady." You just sit down and later on you need to tell me how's my cooking," Betty requested.

"Taste? Me? No work?" asked Shamala as she placed her hand on her chest and looked puzzled.

"No", smiled Betty.

White people are good actually.

Shamala initials thoughts on 'White People' was negative due to influencing word that she received from her family and villagers, when her decision to work with an Italian family spread uncontrollably at her place.

You will be treated like slave. No foods will be given. Are you willing to sleep in the kitchen? They will abuse you if you do something wrong Mala...

But life is full of surprises. From the first day, the only rule that Shamala has to follow was 'No Rule'. Betty and Banso treated her like their own daughter and insisted Shamala to address them as mummy and daddy. She was also given a room which was fully furnished and air-conditioned with new bed, new comforter and new sets of clothes - all for the tiny lady from Perak. Shamala was also requested to dine with them and every day they will enjoy their dinner together as a family.

"What? When? How daddy?"

Shamala rushed to the hospital as she couldn't believe her ears receiving the news that Betty had lost her eyesight.

She was fine in the morning.

With teary red eyes, Banso was leaning on pillar near the reception while going through some papers.

"Daddy...What happened? Mummy was okay in the morning", questions Shamala with stagnant tears waiting to flow over her cheek.

"Mummy was diagnosed with *Hemianopsia,*" Banso sobbed. "She would not be able to see as normal after this. That's what the doctor said Shamala."

"Where are you up to early in the morning dear?" Betty questions with curiosity while watching Shamala in her yellow attire with plaited hair adorned with Jasmine.

"Opssss. Sorry mummy. Did I wake you up?" Shamala feeling guilty over Betty who got awaken suddenly. She continues to creep around on tip toes to avoid making much sound. "By the time I should be at train station but I dozed off mummy.

"Shamala, are you kidding me," Betty looking at the wall clock. "3 o'clock in the morning my dear! Mummy can guess that you are getting ready to temple but why at this time?"

"Hearing the questions, peeping at Betty, Shamala could only smile seeing her mummy's insecurities. Putting her bag on a chair, Shamala walked towards Betty, sitting beside her and caressed her wavy blonde hair and looked into her green shining eyes in the dimly lighted room. Her tear duct starts to be filled with warm liquid. Resistant to gravitational force, a teardrop landed on Betty's hand.

"Shamala, why are you crying? You knew right mummy don't like you getting sad. Stop crying sweetheart," persuaded Betty.

"Mummy, I knew that I can't do anything to cure your eyes. I don't have enough knowledge to find for a cure and I don't have a lot of money but the only thing that I can do for you is to pray for you mummy. I want you to be back to normal as how you used to be. It's unbearable to see you in this condition. It hurts – extremely. Let me go to my lord, my *Muruga*. I want to ask him to give back your eyesight. You don't deserve this. You have a very good heart," Shamala being unstoppable expressing her emotions and deep buried sorrow inside since the first day Betty having the eye disease.

"Oh Shamala, praise the Lord. God is always the best. Now I understand why he sent this little angel to me. My solace in my hard times," Betty murmured. I've never carried you in my womb but your affection and love for me are limitless. Your mother is lucky to have you as her daughter but for the moment I'm the luckiest to have you in my arms. Mummy love you Shamala. Don't worry my dear, as mummy always says, 'Love Heals'. My eyes will heal too."

Besides withstanding the pain and sudden shock in her life, Betty's confidence towards god and life was unshakable.

"I love you mummy. I love you more than anything." Looking straight into the eyes, Shamala hold Betty's hand as tight as possible. "When everyone turned me down, you raised me up by giving your hand. When everyone looked me as a bad omen, you looked me as an angel. I won't let you to be like this mummy. I will go to the end of the earth to bring back my mummy's eye back."

If the walls, ceiling, fan, wardrobe, bed, comforter, hanging clothes and photo frame in the room could express their feeling, looking at both women, the room could be flooded with water.

Shamala really wanted to help Betty. She decided to call her father who used to have a lot of knowledge and ideas about traditional cure. When her father heard of everything, he later suggested that an Indian traditional way of curing which is located near to Shamala's village would be good to give a try. She immediately told Betty and Banso about the news given by her father because she knows the more they delay, the worse the condition could be. Betty and Banso who were really helpless at the moment, immediately agreed to Shamala's suggestions.

So they all went to Shamala's village to meet her family. Her father introduced them to the traditional doctor. Everyday Shamala's father will come and check on Betty and her husband whether they are comfortable with everything there. Shamala accompanied Betty and stayed with her all the time while the treatment was going on. All she wants is Betty to get her eyesight again. So everyday she will go to temple and prays for her employer's eyes as she believe the power of genuine prayer is always unstoppable.

Sun and moon passed and with the endless effort and prayers, the treatment undergone by Betty had been a success. Both Betty and Banso were really grateful to Shamala and her family. So that was the time when they both was about to go back to Italy and that was the time for Shamala to pack her things because Banso wants her to come with them, not just as an helper but as their daughter to Italy- a dream come true moment for a village girl.

This was the first time Shamala going to take a plane for travelling and she have to do it all alone because Betty and Banso left earlier to Brazil due to some pending business work there. Although it was the first time, she was very excited and confident. Everything was very smooth and there come the final part; Boarding into the plane. The officer stopped Shamala and asked her for the boarding pass. She was puzzled as she could not understand what the officer was asking because of poor knowledge in English. Thus, immediately Shamala took her passport and gave it to the officer proudly. The officer stared in horror for few seconds and grinned looking at her. He realized that she must be the first timer to experience all this boarding process. So he decided to help Shamala with her boarding experience. Though it was really embarrassing yet she didn't fail in showing her confident face. She gave a thanking smile to the officer who helped her and off she went. (THE FLIGHT GOES TO ITALY)

5

Yawning.

"Finally 'Sleeping Beauty' is awake," giggled a middle-aged Brazilian man. Sleeping since yesterday aren't you? You must be very tired. Want some drinks?"

Shamala smiled broadly.

"How many hours more for us to reach Italy sir?" Shamala took a peep at the window. "Sir, how high does this airplane flying?

"Around five and forty to forty-five"

Blinked for a second. Tilted her head slightly to take a glance at the man who is sitting beside her.

(Laughing). "You look cute when you do like that sleeping beauty."

Shamala blushes upon hearing the words but still she was waiting for the man to answer her question.

"Ok, actually we will land in five hours' time which means, seven thirty… eight…"

"Twelve thirty!" Shamala answered instantly.

"Yes you are right. And for your second question, we are flying around forty to forty-five thousands feet high from the ground.

"My god. That's really high! Shamala exclaimed.

Not again.

Shamala's tiny eyes met with the same eyes that she tried to avoid yesterday when she boarded the flight.

And now, why is he coming towards me?

"Good morning miss. What would you like to have? Coffee or tea?" with his charming smile, the Singapore Airlines steward asked Shamala.

"Emmmm... I... Coffee will do gentleman." (Smiling quietly).

"Here you go. And anything else?" asked the steward.

"No. No..." stammered Shamala.

Did I just say 'no'? Shamala, can't you hear your tummy grumbling. Why Shamala why?

"Ok, anything just let me know. And you look beautiful when you sleep." The charismatic and good looking steward went off while giving away his compliments. Shamala's face turned red in shyness.

"See I told you that you are a sleeping beauty", again the Brazilian man complimented. "And lady I think that Indian man was having an eye on you. Since yesterday I've been observing him that he was observing you. Something is fishy. (Laughing)

Again she was blushing in shyness but it doesn't last for less than five minutes. As usual, after her energy booster, coffee goes in, she started to fill her journey with questions, stories, jokes and the flight flies smoothly.

"Mummy, daddy," Shamala ran in excitement seeing her employers face.

"I was so worried thinking of you travelling all alone by yourself and it's your first time," worried Betty.

"But I don't." Banso gave a confident look. "I know my little girl is brave and courageous enough for everything. Anyway Shamala, welcome to Italy."

Everything is new to Shamala. This is a dream come true moment for her. How did she end up here? Only god knew the answer.

Dear god, no matter what happens, no matter where I go, I promise, till my last breathe I won't forgot them as my dream would not come to reality without these two lovely souls.

"Beautiful!" Shamala fell in love on her first sight which falls on the gigantic and magnificent ancient Roman Catholic Church at St. Paul and Petro.

"We will come here every Sunday. Is that ok for you?" Banso promised to Shamala who was getting fascinated with the architecture of the church.

"I'll love to papa. I love going to church. I don't know why but whenever I enter into the church, I feel calm and peace. And whenever I see Jesus Christ, without I realize, I'll cry papa. Maybe I'm too attached with stories heard from teachers during my primary school."

"You went to school my dear?" queried Betty. "How did I miss that? I think there is a lot more for mummy to know about you Shamala."

"It would be my pleasure to share about me with you mummy." Shamala gave a warm smile to Betty. "I studied until standard three, in St Joseph primary school, an English medium school. There was where I learnt some words in English and there is also where I started to get attached with Jesus Christ. But after poverty hit my family, eventually I lost interest in studying.

"That's so sad. But I think if you had continued, you would have emerged as best student. You had the potential Shamala," commented Banso while looking at Shamala through the rear view mirror. "Shamala, can daddy ask you something?"

"Sure daddy," assured Shamala.

"I wonder, as an Indian girl how did you develop your love towards Jesus?" asked Banso.

"Simple daddy, I respect all the religion and their belief. I believe respect is the first step for us to express our love. I learnt these when I mingled with my Malay, Chinese and Christian friends. Sometimes I did ask myself why god sent us Buddha, Jesus and Nabi Muhammad. As time passes I understand that they were sent to deliver similar message through different ways. I respect all the messengers who were sent to earth for guiding human being, but whenever I look at Jesus, I felt something special inside me," Shamala finishes with a smile.

Banso was amazed to hear those words from Shamala.

Small by age but the way she sees the world is different.

From the airport to house, Betty shared a lot of information of her country's culture, tradition, heritage, arts and festivals celebrated. After a long drive from the airport, finally they reached their house which was located just beside the St Paul and Peters church.

"Hola Sham", Cloudia and Danialla welcomed Shamala with hugs and kisses. Like their parents, both ladies were so humble that Shamala's initial fear on them subsides eventually.

"You look beautiful Sham, adored Danialla. And younger too", continued Cloudia while looking at her younger sister. Both of them were making jokes of themself as they were big and tall compare to Shamala who is thin and small for her age.

Shamala was overwhelmed with praises and she found it surprising as this was the first time for people to call someone with dark skin as 'Beautiful'. Her memories flooded with her villagers face and hurtful words.

I was not more than a fluff to them.

Suddenly Shamala was stricken with Betty's word; *Don't cling to anything. Clinging is the cause of our being unconscious. The best way to respond to temporary emotion is to ignore it. Keep moving my dear.*

A week passed and Shamala loved her new world. She felt comfortable to get along with her new family members. Her daily routine as usual starts in the morning and ends in the evening. She was instructed to do her jobs only for five days in a week. While in weekends, Shamala was given full freedom to explore her new world – Italy.

"Italy class?" Shamala questions in shock. "But mummy, I felt, I've cost you a lot of expenses. All these clothes and shoes, you bought for me. Not that I'm refusing but I want to buy with my own money. And for the class, I'm so eager and zealous to learn but I want to do it with my own earned money mummy."

"Oh, Shamala, these are the reasons why you were so special to us," praised Betty. "Mummy wants to remind you again, as mummy had told you about this before but just in case that you have forgotten, do not ever downgrade yourself thinking that you are just an helper, who came to work. We brought you here. Till papa and mummy are here, you are and will always be our daughter and of course, as your parents here, we want our child to be in the best condition. As per your wish, you can pay for your things after this but for your Italy class, mummy and daddy will support you financially and you can't say no. This is a request. Can we?"

"God is great mummy. If not because of him, I wouldn't get you in my life. Thank you mummy, thank you daddy. You are the best." Shamala was in tears.

6

"*Hola*", greeted Bravislla wearing his nicest smile. "I don't believe this. Thank god. Finally, you come."

"How can I say no to my best friend in the town," said Shamala with merriment.

Bravislla. Another character in Shamala's life whom she met in train on her way back from her language class. When she was trying to figure out on which route to take for her to get back home, Bravislla who noticed this helped Shamala with the routes and eventually they become friends.

"I still remember your reaction when I invited you to my gallery," Bravislla trying to recall the moment. "Your eyes seem as if it's gonna pop out from your eye socket." (Laughed)

Shamala's face turned red in shyness. She patted Bravislla signaling him to stop laughing at her. "I was so shocked and was thinking of mummy and daddy, whether they will allow me or not. But as usual, they will always let me to do what makes me happy."

"So, now you must agree that I am making you happy", tittered Bravislla. "You knew what Shamala, rather than I'm saying that I'm making you happy, I would definitely say that, whenever you are with me, I felt contented and comfortable. You are one of a kind."

"Okay….Okay… Buddy relax. I knew why you are praising me this lot. You are hungry and you want me to accompany you for lunch. Am I right?"

"Hahahaha…. You are very smart Shamala"

Bravislla took Shamala for a tour to his art's gallery. Shamala was astonished as each picture trying to portray a meaning and the more Shamala look at his drawing, the more she got enthusiastic without she realize. After lunch, both of them went to Bosnia, a metropolitan city with bustling citizens. As usual, Bravislla took his camera out to capture his moments with Shamala.

"Shamala, call for you dear".

"On my way mummy," wild into urgency, Shamala ran towards the hall and took the handset from Betty.

"Hello," breathlessly Shamala answered.

"Hello," a soft voice heard at end of the line.

"*Amma*," Shamala sounded in excitement. "How are you?"

"I'm fine Mala? How about you? All ok?" Kalyani questioning her daughter with full concern.

"All ok *maa* (short form for mother). Don't worry about me. How is everyone there? Is Chinna *anna* fine? Pugazh? Must be repairing something right now," laughed Shamala at end of her continuous questions.

"Everyone is doing good dear and hope you are well and healthy," worried Shamala's mother. Eat well Mala and don't worry about us here. No need to send all your money for us. Keep some for you, and Mala *amma* wants to see you.

Shamala heart started to feel heavy. "I miss you too *amma*. A Lot...."

"And Shamala, before *amma* forget, your sister will get married by end of this year. *Maapillai* (bridegroom) side approved our alliance in one visit dear," Kalyani sharing the happy moment with her daughter. "They said Chellama looks very fair and flawless. You must have seen your sister's face when they praised like that. Whole face started to blush in shyness. Thank god everything went well that day. A lot of work waiting to be done and only you will be missing in the occasion. Okay Mala, *amma* will call you again. Take care and eat well okay. Mala? Are you there?"

"Errrr. Yeah. Yes *amma*", stammered Shamala. "Take care. Happy to hear the good news. Will call you soon too *maa*".

Click. The line went dead.

Heart thumping, lurking in the background, tugging, pulling and cajoling with emotions and at last Shamala uttered a cry of pain, failing to pacify her wild pacing thoughts, sliding via the wall with her back reaching the floor slowly.

Fair and flawless.

These words from her mother were echoing in her drums refusing to leave, torturing her inner-peace and confusing her neurons.

"Shamala," Betty bellowed seeing Shamala sitting on the floor with tears dwelling in her eyes. Betty darted towards Shamala to check on her and sat beside her after getting assurance from Shamala that she is physically fine.

"What happened sweetheart," Betty runs her hand over Shamala's long, wavy and silky-thick hair.

Shamala sobbed quietly into the shoulders of Betty. "Why mummy, god punish me this harsh. I don't understand why. It hurts a lot. I knew, *amma* was unintentional, but when I think back, at end of the day, skin colour was set as a parameter to approve a marriage alliance. If only fair girls will get married, then how about girls like me mummy? Aren't we eligible to get married? Somehow I have to go back home right? And *amma* will be trying so hard to fix alliance for me right? Since small mummy, till now, I was judged as 'ugly'. I feel very sad mummy."

"No Shamala, no," Betty trying to convince her. "Constantly fretting on something will turn your thoughts dark. Sometimes in life, unexpected and stressful events, words, people or whatever it is, could sometimes leave us feeling overwhelmed and emotionally beaten, bruised and battered. But we must remember that our character is formed by the challenges that we face and overcome. Our courage grows when we face our fears. Our strength and our faith are built as we get tested in our life experiences. Now tell mummy, what makes us strong?"

(Deep silence)

"Problems", answered Shamala.

"Good girl. What do we get when we face our problems," questioned Betty again with a warm smile.

"Strong.... We become strong mummy".

"Exactly!" See I knew that my girl is strong and brave. Once, during my meltdown, she was the one stood beside me, consoling my soul and instilled confidence in me. Remember that girl?" Betty looking into Shamala eyes who is trying to recollect her moments during Betty's eye operation.

Little smile blossomed on Shamala's face.

"Thank god. My daughter had smiled," Betty hugged Shamala. "Dear, again mummy reminding you that, you must get rid of body shaming or appearance shaming from your mind and heart. To ease you with the process, let mummy tell you a short story. Have you heard about *Black Beauty*?"

"*Black Beauty*? No mummy," replied Shamala softly.

"Okay. It is a story written in year 1877 by an English author named Anna Sewell. Wondering how mummy remembered the year, it was the year when my mummy was born, and she was the one who told me that story," Betty giving a big smile to Shamala. "So what so special about the story is, back in 1877, humans and horses had a totally different relationship than they do today. For those who want to go somewhere, they only two options; A steam engine or a horse. But at the time, much of the general public wasn't really aware that horses needed to be treated differently than steam engines. The whole story is narrated by a titular horse named Black Beauty. As his name suggests, he was prized for his size and strength. But when misfortune comes, he is sold to a series of different owners. Some handlers are kind and showed him love and respect. Others are careless or worse-callous. When Black Beauty is rode hard over dark roads by a drunken groom, he stumbles, loses a shoe and injures his legs. Though still beautiful, he is less valuable and ends up in London, pulling a carriage through teaming, dirty streets — a far cry from the green meadows of his youth."

Shamala was listening attentively to Betty's story.

"This story is very close to my heart because, it is hard to find purpose or good in difficult circumstances, but that is the journey. People will judge you, criticize you, comment on you and the worst, they will hurt you but the way we bounce back after we are being pushed down will prove how much we love ourselves. Yes! Sometimes we need a break. A break where you can take to learn on solutions rather than problems," Betty finishing her story while fondly looking at Shamala. "Life is simple my dear once you start to love it from inside, no one could stop from outside. And black is not just a colour. It is an emotion. You want to know something Shamala? You are very beautiful; Sparkling black eyes, pointed nose, cute reddish lips and perfect brown skin with curvy body shape. Not everyone is blessed to get what you got. And Sham, a real man will see you from his heart not from his eyes. I am sure that one day you will meet the one who really deserve you and the one who will not judge you. Mark my words dear. Love is magic. You will understand this when you see your magician."

"Shall we go back?" Shamala carrying her handbag, indicating it's time for them to go back home.

Marco who was drowned in the story immediately came to real life and nodded his head, agreeing to Shamala's request. Marco was about to ask more as he was really attracted with Shamala's life journey, but realizing that Roberta will be waiting for them, he decided to pause his questions for the moment.

7

It's Valentine's Day. Synonymous with love, Italians traditionally have been considered to be lovers. Known in Italy's as 'La Festa Degli Innamorati', Valentine's Day is only celebrated between lovers. Young sweethearts in Italy profess their love for each other by giving flowers, chocolates and beautiful gifts.

Dear god, nothing could be compared to the pain you endured for the sake human being. Whenever I think about you, my sorrows turn into strength, and for the life I'm living now, it is a blessing. I know, thanking you won't be enough for what you've given me. As return I want to do something, and my heart urges me to be a 'Nun'. Please show me the path for me to serve people in need.

Shamala paused and lit candle. She held it close to her body, as if she didn't want to take too much space. Warmness from the candle flame and deep silence in the church soothes Shamala's mind and soul.

"Bless me Father", requested Shamala upon seeing Father Joseph.

"May god bless you my child. Aren't you celebrating your Valentine's my dear?"

"Yes, I am celebrating Father," pointing her finger to Jesus, "The love of my life."

Father Joseph smiled hearing to Shamala's words.

"Father, I've made my mind to become a nun, but I'm not sure on the process. Could you help me with that Father?" Shamala questioned.

"Certainly my dear," replied Father. "But not now, I'll let you know shortly when you have to attend for the courses."

"Thank you Father."

Everything around Shamala seems to be moving in fast-forward and slow motion at the same time. It was her 10th time, taking a glance at the church entrance looking for Bravislla's shadow.

For god sake, where is this guy?

A hand closed on Shamala's shoulder.

Finally.

Shamala turned to give a dismay look at Bravislla. (Shamala's eye went big)

Who is he?

Shamala did a bewildered three-sixty, scanning for some sort of clue. "*Hola*, how may I help you?"

"*Hola belle,* Happy Valentine's Day. This is for you," the young charming man handed a bouquet of red roses to Shamala. (Again Shamala's eyes get big).

"Thank you gentleman, it's very beautiful".

"Not more than you sweetheart," replied him.

Okay. I think he is not okay. Shamala be alert.

With the loveliest smile that she could give, Shamala looked at the young man again, "Thank you for the compliment and if you don't mind, may I know who are you?"

"Opss. I'm so sorry. Forget to introduce myself. My name is Danielle."

"Ohww, nice name," complimented Shamala.

"And I'm in love with you," the young man expressed.

"What!"

(Again her eyes went big but this time it is really big)

"No, I won't agree for this. How can I give her to someone she didn't know before Banso?"

"Betty, I understand that you are worried on her safety, but somehow, one day she needs to get married right. Think about her mother at village how happy she would be if she found that her daughter received a marriage proposal from a prince lineage family," Banso trying to persuade his wife.

Giving a sharp look at Banso, "You thought that I didn't think of that. Come on Banso, of course I knew how the mother would feel, but we must realize that, for the time being we are Shamala's guardian. We have to think from all angles regarding this proposal dear. We can't simply say yes to their proposal. Danialle came from royal family. Even though they seem to be sweet but we have to enquire. It requires time and I have to talk to her mother and sister about this too."

"Okay, then take your time. They didn't urge us to give reply soon. We will settle this together dear. I believe Shamala's noble heart that made god to send a prince to take of our princess. She deserves to be happy, and you wished that all the time. Am I right?" Banso putting his hand around Betty's shoulder trying to calm his worried wife.

Shamala returned to awareness through a dense fog and a pounding headache. After midnight, Shamala lay in bed, trying to stop her brain for bringing back all the memories alive. Rather than being free after sharing what's buried inside, the deep conversation with Marco last night actually rekindled moments which she tried to forget years ago.

Why did he come in my life? It hurts Danielle.

[Three….. Two…..One…..]

Happy birthday to you,
Happy birthday to you,
Happy birthday to Shamala
Happy birthday to you.

(Claps filling the celebration)

"Wait, wait. Don't blow," Roberta stopped Shamala from cutting the cake. "Close your eyes, make a wish, then take out the candle from the cake. Don't blow out the candle."

Shamala gives a thumb up for Roberta's words. Her eyelids went down, fingers brought together, placed close to her heart, Chest moving up and down while drawing air in and out accompanied with wishes. Chatters from surrounding could be heard clearly but there was a deep silence inside.

Ding Dong!

Ding Dong!

"I'll get the door," Marco running towards the living room.

That was when Shamala's gaze fixed on a figure at the door - and all too – familiar wheelchair bearing a grown man holding a bouquet of lavender.

"Gian Franco!" Shamala exclaimed.

"Can I come in?" asked the man at the door.

"Oh my god, I'm sorry Gian. Come in," invited Shamala who went speechless for a couple of seconds.

Marco's eyeball went left and right witnessing the moment between them. "Let me help you *fratello* (brother)," Marco lifting the back wheel of the wheelchair to ease Gian Franco to get in.

"*Grazie fratello* (thanks brother). I'm Gian Franco, Shamala's friend."

"I'm Marco, Shamala's brother. Nice to meet you." Both gentleman shook hands.

"This is for you," Gian Franco giving the bouquet to Shamala. "Happy birthday dear."

"You never missed my birthday Gian," Shamala started to shed her tears. "Where did you go? Did you know how much I missed I you? I went all the places trying to find you, but all my effort went vain."

"I'm sorry sweetheart. It's..." Gian unable to complete his sentence. "I didn't mean do that. One minor surgery at UK. After that, I stayed there for some years and just came back last week."

"Surgery! When, um … why?" Shamala spluttered.

"Yeah surgery," nodded Gian Franco. "Surgery for my legs. Now I'm okay, don't worry."

"I'll get drinks for both of you," Marco went away giving space for two long lost friends to chat.

Shamala strolled towards Gian and kneeled down beside his wheelchair. "Is your leg really okay now? What happened? What did the doctor say? Any chances for you to walk again?"

With a big smile, Gian placed his finger at Shamala's chin, tilting her face upwards, trying to look into her black tiny eyes. "You never change. The same kindness, love and care. Nothing changed in you except for your eyes. Something is missing in these lovely eyes."

"Only changes do not change Gian," Shamala giving a bitter smile. "I've changed. Changes that made me to sustain in my life," she sighed. "Forget about me. Somehow I'm good. With Roberta's and Marco's presence, I'm happy."

"Sorry to interrupt. There you go, freshly brewed coffee for both of you. You guys carry on. Anything just let me know ok." Marco moving to the dining hall once again.

"I'm happy to know that you are happy Shamala." Gian Franco taking a sip of coffee and finishes the uneasy topic. He noticed Shamala's fake smile too, trying to hide something from him.

"Forget to ask you Gian, how is mother?" asked Shamala.

"She is great dear. Besides taking care of herself, she needs to take of 'this' grown burden too. Sometimes I do wonder what I will do without my iron lady."

"Don't say like that Gian. You are her strength, and she is your support," Shamala patted Gian's back. "And … How is he?"

"He…? Who…?" Gian trying to provoke Shamala, even he knew who she is trying to enquire.

"Don't give me that look Gian. I knew that you know who I'm trying to enquire about."

Gian took a deep breath to answer this question. "He's good".

"Good to hear that he is good," Shamala said glumly.

"Just go away from my life Danielle. We are not meant for each other. 'You and I'. We come from two different worlds. Your culture and mine are totally different." Shamala uttering a cry of pain, as if she'd been pricked with a thorn.

"No. I won't. I knew I'm wrong, but it is not fair for me. Don't I deserve a second chance? Everyone makes mistake but they got opportunity to rectify their mistake. Please *belle*, just one last chance." Danielle kneeling down while holding Shamala hands tightly.

Shamala couldn't face her fiancée. "Get up Danielle. You don't have do this. For your status and wealth, sure someone can replace my place."

"But … no one could be you", he stammered.

"Stop it Danielle. Get up. Don't make me to feel bad as I'm already feeling bad," bellowed Shamala in tense.

"I won't," howled Danielle.

"You have to, because you have no choice," shouted Shamala. "You should have thought of this before you sleep with another woman. You knew how much I suffered after seeing you with that woman at my bed to be. I felt like hell. I felt like dying. You won't know this feeling because, I've said before, the way that you and I were raised are totally different. Just leave me and go away from my life".

Danialle stood up upon hearing Shamala's words. He gets one of Shamala's hands and placed their engagement ring on her hand which she threw on his face after that incident. "I'm sorry… Deep down from my heart, I really regret for what I've done to the love of my life. I'm sorry *belle*. Extremely sorry. Maybe I don't understand why this happened to us but keep this in your mind; you will always be my wife. No one could change that in my life. Take care dear. I love you."

He leaves Shamala standing with the ring on her hand trying to digest his words with tears accompanying her thoughts.

"Nooooo," screamed Shamala hearing a tiny vehicle screeched to a halt behind after hitting the man who she asked to go away a few minutes ago. She turned on the jets, knees pumping like pistons. She was still losing ground. Athletic she was, her legs were shorter, her lung capacity smaller. A detonation of pure adrenaline galvanized her into action. The more she ran towards Danialle, the more she felt guilty for letting him to go away.

Heartbeat drops, thoughts went blank and her knees went weak, collapsing beside her fiancée who is lying on a pool of blood.

Mornings were the hardest for Shamala, even worse than the regretting sleepless of nighttime. Morning was when she had to lurch out of an exhausted slumber, only to remember yet again the awful truth of what happened past few days ago.

The routine was always the same. She would get dressed and join Betty and Banso in pushing scrambled eggs around a plate. Betty invariably burned the toast, but no one complained. No one had intention of eating it anyway.

10

"Good night Shamala."

"Good night Gian. Hope you don't go missing again after this," smiled Shamala.

"No, I won't," Gian assured. We'll meet again." Gian's car left, leaving Shamala standing at the front. Her birthday ends with a surprise which she didn't expect and old memories came flooding back. It was really ironic when Shamala reminds herself how she met Gian for the first time as Danielle introduced him as his best buddy to her.

"Hai," Shamala made her first move to introduce herself to Danielle's friend, Gian Franco who was sitting in a wheelchair. He felt really shy to face Shamala

Noticing this, without hesitating, Shamala immediately shake hand with him accompanied with her sweet smile. That's how their first meeting went and day after that, every time when Shamala go out with

Danielle, Gian will be there too and three of them used to share a lot of stories.

"How long have you been using wheelchair Gian?" Shamala's first question to Gian.

He was not a wheel chair user since birth but it happened after getting high fever during his teenage years. Although life was hard, he did not gave up and attended all therapies since the doctors gave him hope that he will be back to normal as before. Shamala was really touched and also inspired with Gian's story

Who knows that that was a real last time she met him as Danielle accident made her life upside down for a long time. She did not expect that she would meet Gian again in her life. Shamala felt grateful for meeting him as there must be a purpose of God sending him in her life again.

11

Shamala was really excited as Gian's party was around the corner. She wanted to cook something special for him.

"I will make *palgoa* (Indian sweet) and vegetarian briyani for him," Shamala delightfully started her cooking.

Shamala tied her *saree* and for the first time she was trying the Indian traditional attire. When she saw herself at mirror, she remembered those old boyish days where how hard her mother will force her to tie saree but she will not compromise with her since she don't like to dress up like a girl.

Marco and Shamala was quite late to the party and they wanted to give a surprise since Gian did not know they had fly back to Italy few days ago after visiting few places at London.

"Tadaaaaa……," Marco and Shamala at Gian's house entrance.

"I thought both of you were in London. Anyway thank you for coming," Gian got surprised as he did not expect that Shamala will turn up to the party. He did not blink his eyes after seeing her in traditional attire with her beautiful smile. She gave Gian a small hug.

"How are you doing few days without me," Shamala trying to divert Gian's eyes which are continuously staring her.

The party started after all the guest arrived. Everyone took their place at the dining table except for Shamala as she didn't have chair to sit down. One of Gian's friends uttered something in Spanish and everybody started to laugh except for Shamala as she did not understand what they were talking about. Gian cheeks turned red and he immediately offered Shamala to company her to take their dinner outside. Everyone present there laughed once again.

Smiling with curiosity, Shamala asked, "Why they all are laughing Gian?"

Gian who could not stop smiling, looked at Shamala with a cute hesitation, "They said, you don't need a chair as you have my lap to sit on."

Shamala's jaws fell down.

"I'm sorry. They were just joking. Don't take it too seriously okay." Gian trying to convince Shamala when there was a change in her face reaction. "Every time they will insist me to bring you to meet them, as I used to talk about you. So they got excited when they meet you."

Shamala patted Gian's back as a sign of okay with the incident which happened at the dining hall. She did not take it very seriously because strangely she liked it. After so long, her heart feels light. Both of them went out and settled at a small cozy space. They kept silence for quite some time.

"Do you want to try the *palgoa*?" Shamala offered.

"Yeah sure. You made them?" asked Gian.

"Why, won't you eat if I say I made them," Shamala chuckled.

"Hahahaha, okay, I'm eating." Gian ate the *palgoa* and he really loved it. "The *palgoa* is very scrumptious and sweet as you this evening Shamala," Gian's praised.

His words made Shamala to blush and laugh at the same time.

"Shamala I have to admit that I really fell for you since the first time I saw you in the Church but I did not have the confidence to tell it to you because I am disabled person and not normal like others. You always told me that I am overqualified to be your friend but now I believe that I am qualified to be your life partner," Gian ended his deep buried words and passed something to Shamala

"Nice to hear these words from you. I felt grateful and loved at the same time. But before that, always remember that you are not disabled. You are differently abled Gian. I always felt blessed to have you by my side," Shamala smiled.

Then when Marco interrupted; "*Bambola* we need to go back. *Mamma* called."

"Oh okay. Let's go back home. I need to give medicine too," told Shamala.

Shamala left without replying anything to Gian's words. When Shamala was in the car, she opened the crumbled paper that Gian gave and there was a wedding ring inside it. The crumbled paper was a sketch of their wedding card and there was a small note saying;

Don't get me started about love and affection.
For it's a long story.
I haven't lost my heart to a stranger.
It's a friend who has done this favour.
I will wait for the princess of my heart.

Seeing this, Shamala could not stop grinning. She understands the whole situation where Gian told his friends all his plans before Shamala arrive to the party. She remembered the one who did the joke at dinner table as she asked not to disappoint Gian when Shamala shook hand with her before she leaves. She also told her that Shamala is very important in his life.

"*Momma*" shouted Marco when he saw Roberta was lying down on the floor.

"Mom… Can you hear me? Wake up…. Please don't do this to me," Marco spluttered

As there was no sign of waking up from Roberta, they immediately rushed her to the hospital. Hours passed. The doctors came out from the Intensive Care Unit (ICU).

"She had major heart attack. Keep praying for her," the doctor left Marco and Shamala in silence.

"No! This is not happening," wept Marco.

Shamala glanced back at Marco, who has collapsed on the couch, an expression of disbelief on his pale features.

After a few weeks of observation, Marco's mother was allowed to go back home or more to say to bring her back home as she was still in a coma mode. They hired a nurse and set up all the necessary hospital equipment for her.

There was endless prayer from Shamala; day and night as she really wanted Roberta to get well soon. At the same time, Shamala was really helpless because she wanted to meet and reply Gian but due to Roberta's worsening condition, she don't have the heart to leave her alone

"Ahhhhhhh," a loud voice heard from Roberta room that made Shamala to run immediately to her room. Roberta was mumbling louder and louder from time to time. Shamala was overwhelmed and immediately she called Marco.

"Marco, come home now! *Mamma* is talking. She is out from coma," burst Shamala. She had no idea how she was shouting loudly on the phone line.

Dup ...! Shamala dropped her phone with her jaw dropped and eyes enlarged, she saw Roberta's leg was turning purple black without blood circulation and slowly it went up through her whole body. By the time, her face turned pale and white eventually. Her mumbling stopped, and there was no sign of breathing. Shamala's tears were unstoppable as she saw death with her own eyes and seeing Roberta lying as a corpse in front of her.

By the time Marco arrived, everything has ended. Marco was in tears and he looked worst. Shamala had never seen him crying that much and she felt something wrong. He right away hugged her tightly.

"Shamala, your mother is also no more. Just now I received a call from your brother regarding of your late mum," he wailed.

The next moment Shamala did not know what happened. She collapsed in Marco arm.

It had been two weeks after the tragedy happened and life become more pathetic when Shamala can't go back Malaysia immediately because there was no flight ticket available. Although she was broke into pieces, She still stood beside Marco during the last rituals for Marco's mum.

Marco did not call anyone to conduct any of the rituals. He did it all by himself including carrying his mum body to the bathroom, giving bath, preparing the coffin and the whole night, Marco slept beside his mom's coffin and did not let anybody to came near him including Shamala.

12

It was wonderful morning and Shamala was busy cleaning the praying place, to make sure it looks tidy and clean before her employer arrives and starts his daily routine at factory with prayers.

"*Kaacheh* (elder sister in Chinese)," called Ton while searching for the wonder woman of his factory.

I wonder what work she is doing right now.

Ton sighed with a smile thinking of Shamala who won't stop a minute for leisure.

"Kaacheh... Kaacheh," yelled Ton after not getting any response from Shamala.

"Yes Ton. I'm coming." Shamala run towards Ton with jiggling laughters. "Aiyaah! What happened?"

"There you are *kaacheh.* Good morning and here you go all the needed items for prayers. Could you please conduct the prayers as I urgently need to meet an important client this morning? Since yesterday that client was pestering me for a discussion on quotation for chrome plating. So, I need to go now and I'll meet you around 1 p.m." Ton left hurriedly with a big hopeful smile after handing over the responsibility to his favorite sister, Shamala.

'Ton and Shamala'. Employer and employee for the world but brother and sister by heart. Despite different race, religion and culture, there was a deep, lovable, mutual understanding and respect between the two souls. During Ton's hard times, Shamala used to be the pillar of strength for him. No matter how big the problem was for Ton during his learning days at his uncle's factory, Shamala was the only one who instills confidence and courage for him to believe that problems are only passing clouds.

Ding Dong!

Ding Dong!

Ding Dong!

Siapaan tuu? (Who is that?)

Siti sighed hearing the factory bell keep on ringing

Ding Dong!

"*Nanti* (wait)," darted Siti impatiently heading to the gate feeling irritated with the bell.

"Aunty is *periamma* in?" asked a teenage girl by the gate.

"Aikk Kanmani. *Masuk, masuk. Periamma ada. Kejap aunty panggil ya* (Aikk Kanmani. Come in, come in. *Periamma* is in. Wait, I'll call her)," Siti running inside to call Shamala.

"*Kak Mala, Kanmani kat luar (It's Kanmani waiting out there Mala sister),*" informed Siti.

Seeing her niece with a piece of paper in her hand and teary red eyes, Shamala hurried to get her in her arms.

"Don't cry my dear. You had worked day and night for this. So, now it's time to accept what we have reaped, Shamala consoled.

Kanmani was still speechless while hugging her aunt.

"Let *periamma* see dear," requested Shamala to see her niece's SPM examination result.

"*Andeverey* (oh god), one, two, three .... Ten! Ten A's." Shamala could not believe her eyes.

Shamala was jumping in euphoria. Now it's her turn to be speechless. She could not control her tears. Again both of them hugged each other tightly, not allowing air to pass through them.

"Thank you *periamma*. This is the least that I can do to make you happy for all that you have done for me," sobbed Kanmani while looking into the tired eyes of her hardworking aunt. "This couldn't have happened without you *periamma*."

"No dear. It's your hard work," Shamala praised. You did this all by yourself. *Periamma* did nothing but today I really felt proud of you Kanmani."

Seeing both niece and aunt expressing their love, some of the workers shed some tears too.

"*Periamma*, I need to go now. *Amma* is eagerly waiting at home to console me," Kanmani giggled.

"Console you?"

"Yes, yes. Console me because I bluffed to her saying that I got two B's in my exam," Kanmani continue to cackle.

"Hahahaha, you naughty girl. Better get going. Poor *amma*. She must be very worried thinking of you," Shamala cooed.

"Okay *periamma* catch you later and I love you *periamma*," said Kanmani.

"*Periamma* love you too and wait let *periamma* put the result slip inside a plastic cover." Shamala walk towards her desk to find a plastic cover and realized it's raining outside. "It's pouring outside dear. How will you go?"

"No worries periamma. I have umbrella", Kanmani answered.

Off Kanmani went, running all the way from her aunt's factory just to see her mother's unimaginable reaction.

That girl proved that hurdles and obstacles are the stepping stones to achieve success. May god bless her always.

Thinking of all the moments relating to her youngest sister, Kaaviya who came to her place with two little daughters after her husband's demise. Standing at the bus station, with numbing coldness due to long hours of journey in bus, the two little angels, aged four and nine were looking anxiously for Shamala appearing nowhere saying 'Hi'.

Wow! Nine years had passed. Life is too short to regret.

13

"Hello. We are calling from I Mall. Is this Ms. Shamala?"

"Yes. I am. Who is this?" Shamala answered.

"Hai miss, I'm Behta Force supervisor speaking. Sorry to inform you that Kaaviya had fainted at workplace. Could you come over to bring her back home?"

"What? How? When? Is she okay?" Shamala starts to get panic.

"Few minutes ago miss," answered the supervisor. "Her colleagues told that she was okay in the morning but after finishing her patrolling duty around the mall, she was found fainted inside the office room. Don't worry, as now she is still under conscious but it will be better if you bring her back home."

"Okay… I'm coming there now. Please take care of her. I'll reach there shortly," pleaded Shamala.

"Sure miss. Don't worry. We will take care of her for the moment," assured Kaaviya's supervisor.

Oh god. Why must she face hardship again and again?

"Kaaviya… Kaaviya…." Shamala patted her sister's face, awaking her to gain conscious. "Kaaviya open your eyes and see me. Say something."

"Mala," Kaaviya started to cry loudly.

Seeing her sister tears flowing drastically, Shamala could sense that her sister is experiencing some pain but she's unsure of what happened. "Kaaviya, I know. Something is wrong with you but you've to tell me. We'll go to the doctor. Don't worry. Come on. Tell me. Why? Headache? Feeling dizzy?"

"No Mala. I…I…" Kaaviya stammered. "I couldn't see." (Kaaviya crying continuously)

"What!" Shamala in disbelief.

Something is blocking my eyes. I couldn't see Mala. I couldn't see anything Mala. What will I do after this? I don't want to be a burden to you anymore. I don't know how, but I couldn't see Mala. I couldn't see anything". Kaaviya wiping her tears, while trying to enlarge her eyes using her fingers believing she could see something. But to her vain, she only could see a blurry white image.

(After three months)

"Hold my hand tightly, we will go one by one okay," Shamala reminds her sister so that she won't trip over the staircase. It was very difficult for Kaaviya to resume her daily life after her eye surgery but when her pillar of strength was always there holding her tightly preventing her from falling down made her to be strong in facing the current test given by god

"Five more steps and we will reach our house," encourages Shamala.

"Only five?"

"Certainly," answered Shamala with a smile.

Both women reached the house feeling exhausted after the long tiring day at hospital. "You want anything to eat Kaaviya?"

"No Mala, I just want to lie down. Feeling so tired," answered Kaaviya.

Shamala leads her sister to the room and helped her to lie down on the bed. "Anything, call me okay. I'll be outside. Sleep well." Shamala left her sister to take rest while she went to the living room to take a short nap after being sleep deprived for three days.

While at the room, Kaaviya was being unable to close her eyes as she was wrestling with unwanted thoughts out of her mind.

Why must I trouble her again and again. She had done her lot and until now she is doing something for me. I wonder when and how would I pay these kindness debt. Not everyone is blessed to get sister like her. I'm blessed. Dear god, I'm able to withstand anything, doesn't matter whether its sickness or test, but please keep her happy. No harm should not fall on her. Fill her life with happiness.

Faith in prayers continues and as time passes Kaaviya's eye condition improved with the help of modern technology and medicine and not to forget, her deep belief in god.

14

Rhea, help me to pass the leaves. Two leaves once while I'll hang it".

"Ok done." Rhea giving thumbs up to her elder sister Kanmani.

Five hours left for Indian all around the world to celebrate the festival of lights. Shamala was busy grinding overnight left soaked rice and *urad dhall* to prepare batter for breakfast tomorrow while watching two ladies decorating house with earthen Two ladies decorating house with earthen lamps and decorative lights were put in and around giving an atmosphere of joy and happiness. The presence of gaiety, cheerfulness, merrymaking and fun, filled every corner of the house.

"These days Deepavali celebration is very different from those days," Shamala started with her childhood Deepavali stories again. Those days, on Deepavali eve, it would be like a celebration filled with peoples, laughters, pile of works, tiredness but still the excitement had never decrease. Girls will be busy with cooking while boys will be busy with decoration. And you know what, our house will receive the most number of Deepavali cards and every year, different type of card arrangement will be done on the wall. Emmm… It's something that this generation could never experience. We are sorry for that.

"If we can feel the atmospheres on those days, must be very excited right?" Rhea confessing her wish.

Shamala smiled hearing the words from her niece.

"And *periamma,* we have something for you this Deepavali," Kanmani finishing her words while looking at Rhea. Both of them gave a look as if they were hiding a secret.

Shamala looked curiously at the girls, "Something for me, what was that?"

"I don't know how you will accept this, but we wanted to do this. We are unsure whether you will like or dislike this decision but…" Rhea started to give some clues.

"Okay. Enough of suspense. Come on tell me. What's the matter," requested Shamala.

"Actually…" Kanmani started.

"Yeah, physically, biologically, chemically. Enough dude. Spit it out. Somehow she needs to know this," Rhea countered Kanmani.

"Why don't you tell? You are the one who arranged for this right?" said Kanmani.

Shamala was still looking curiously at both of them. "Arranged for what girls?"

"Vacation to Italy." Rhea spilled.

"Seriously," Shamala couldn't believe what she heard a few seconds ago. "But why suddenly?"

"Actually we had been planning for this since early June and Uncle Gian Franco was part of the plan too. We will be going for this coming Christmas; You, amma, akka and me," Rhea explained briefly.

Gian Franco…

Shamala mind clouded with memories came flooding back hearing the name: Journey to Italy, Danielle's proposal, Gian's introduction, engagement, Danielle's accident, Betty and Banso went to Brazil, staying with Marco, Gian appearing after went missing for years, Marco's mother passed away and returning to Malaysia.

"Shamala, is this realy you?"

Gian's voice in the speaker was so close, so clear, that it sounded like it was being beamed straight into her brain. That evening was still fresh. The evening where she talked to Gian Franco after 25 years and all thanks to Rhea and her friend, Tino who took effort to contact each and every Italian number in her aunt's contact book, and fortunately, the last call they made was answered and it was Gian Franco' mother.

What do you think their reaction would be when they meet each other?

"Emmmm", Rhea trying to figure out answer for Kanmani's question while gazing at sceneries outside the window.

Kanmani stared at her sister before starting to fill her mind again with her imaginations on her aunt's reaction when see meet Gian Franco after years passed.

"Oikkk," Kanmani disturbs her sister again.

"Bored is it?" Rhea put her hand phone aside.

"No, but kind of excited. We have heard periamma's story since you and I were kids, and now we gonna walk into our childhood stories in real. We didn't imagine that these all would happen but in reality it is happening.

Giving the most sincere smile, Rhea agreed to Kanmani's words.

As the planner of this vacation to Italy, Rhea was the most excited person at the beginning but once she boards into the plane, her feelings went feeling less. Quite unsure on the reason, but certainly, deep down she felt very happy in bringing her aunt for a vacation to her most favorite place in the world and of course to meet her long lost friend.

"Chill *kaa*. After this you will see more and for sure you will get tired of getting excited." Rhea trying to control her excited sister.

"Heeeee," Kanmani showing her teeth to Rhea. "I'm excited."

After 13-hours journey, at last they reached Italy to have a good time after years of working and handling all sorts of challenges. Besides the desire to go around the historical city, Rhea and Kanmani couldn't wait to see the most anticipated moment of their aunt's life. Years of separation and thousands of memories to be rekindled.

"I saw him."

Remaining 6 eyes went left and right, finding for a figure that Rhea had spotted.

I saw him too.

Shamala's leg grounded on the floor. She could not neither to move or speak.

"*Periamma* that is uncle Gian right? "Kanmani trying to confirm while pointing at a man sitting on wheelchair with a board stating;

'Welcome Again Shamala and family'

"Yes it is uncle Gian," confirmed Shamala. Slowly with her luggage and three ladies accompanying her, she strolled towards her friend whom she hasn't met for long time. "Gian," called Shamala.

The man was busily reading a magazine, stopped for a moment to look at the figure that called his name and found that his old friend was standing and smiling in front of him. A moment of silence could be sensed between the souls. "Finally, you are here again Shamala," Gian voice was shaking when he uttered the words. Tears were dwelling in his eye well. Shamala kneel down beside Gian Franco as how she always used to do twenty five years ago. Holding his hand, "I thought that I won't be able to meet you, but as usual god has different plan dear. I missed you so much. Both of them hugged and cried continuously.

"*Kaa... Kaa,*" Rhea wakes her sister who was found to be in deep sleep. "*Kaa*!" Rhea shook much harder this time as no response received from Kanmani.

Half opened. Then closed. Again opened half and finally she managed to open her eyes fully to check what's happening around her. "We still haven't reach?" Kanmani detangling her messy hair with her finger while stretching her neck to left and right to get rid of her neck stiffness.

That was a beautiful dream.

Kanmani visualizes the moments in her dream where her aunt and her friend meets after decades.

The airport terminal was very busy with passengers coming in many others leaving, there is constant movement of both people and planes.

The aircraft belonging to Singapore Airlines had just landed. As the Boeing slowed down considerably, it glided from one end of the runaway to the other. With so many planes landing, it was difficult to keep track of that one plane continuously. Sometimes it disappeared and then appeared from a fleet of aeroplanes. Many maneuvers later, it took that one final turn and started moving towards the airport terminal, towards the departure side. By now, the speed had reduced to a crawl. A man dressed in an orange work wet guided the plane to its rightful spot, vigorously signaling with lighted batons he held in his hands.

In the meanwhile, even before the aircraft was visible from the building an announcement had already been made, about its arrival. Gian broke the news of the aircraft arrival to his mother. There was a lot of excitement in the air and in Gian's heart too.

Shamala and her family get up from their seats and gathered their belongings. By the time the aircraft had reached the building, people had formed a long queue near the designated boarding gate. Everyone had their hand baggage with them and their boarding passes in their hand, ready to show it to the officials. Another announcement was made, to allow senior citizens, expecting mothers and ladies with children, to board the plane. Everyone made way for them.

As the staff at the counter checked the boarding passes, one mobile staircase each was attached to the front and rear doors of the plane. Soon enough, three buses rolled in. People got into the buses where some sat, while other stood holding on the handles and bars for support.

After collecting their luggages, Shamala eye did a bewildered scan for Gian's figure. "There he is," Shamala pointing to the left corner of the waiting area. "Come girls, let's go."

"*Hola*, greeted Shamala while putting her luggage aside and hugged Gian's mother tightly. "How are you? Oh my god, how long it has been since I saw this lovely face. Then Shamala turns to Gian who was sitting with full smile on his face." I'm back," Shamala hugged Gian. "I missed you a lot. How are you?"

"I'm fine dear. How are you?" Gian's turn to enquire his friend.

As always, I'm good. Feeling very happy to see you like this Gian, smart and tough even after years passed," Shamala smiled, finishing her sentence. "And, yeah, this is Kaaviya, my youngest sister.

"Hai," Kaaviya did a friendly hand shake with Gian.

And these two are her daughters, the eldest is Kanmani and the youngest one is Rhea.

"Hola, *Kan…many*," Gian giggled after pronouncing the name. Kanmani laughed hearing her name pronounced stylishly.

"*Hola* uncle. So nice to meet you in real after hearing your name for years since I'm was little girl, said Kanamani.

"Oh really, I've been that famous in your house," Gian started to joke with Kanmani. "And this tall girl must be Rhea right?"

"Yes I am," Rhea smiled when Gian didn't go wrong with her name. "Very happy to see you uncle. You look exactly the same as in what I saw in your profile picture. A bit old but handsome."

Gian laughed to his heart content hearing Rhea words. Indeed he agrees on what Rhea commented.

Time passes super-fast.

"Okay come everyone, let's go back home. You all must be very tired. Once we reach home, all of you can freshen up yourself, rest for a while and then we will go out for dinner. Is that okay?" Gian arranging the schedule for his long distance guest.

Temperature shows eighty degree. After lunch, Gian brought the ladies from Malaysia for sightseeing around Rome.

"I think I've seen this fountain somewhere but I couldn't remember where," Kanmani trying to loosen her memory knots to retrieve at where she has seen the Trevi Fountain. "Oh I know, *periamma's* photo album. Right? She would be sitting with her legs crossed.

Shamala smiled as a sign of agree to Kanmani's guess. "You can make a wish by throwing a coin into the water," raved Shamala. "Go girls. Make a wish".

"Aren't you following?" asked Rhea.

"No dear, I'll be here with uncle Gian. You all carry on," said Shamala.

"Okay, we will be back soon," Rhea elbowed her sister signaling her to follow her.

Watching the ladies strolling towards the fountain, Shamala settled beside Gian who seems to be drowning in deep thoughts.

"Gian," Shamala trying to break the silence present.

"Years back, I made a wish too, but unfortunately, until now my wish was never granted. Maybe I'm not good in making wish," a voice of dismay breaking the silence.

Now Shamala went into deep thoughts trying to digest Gian's sentences.

"Not everyone is lucky enough for their wishes to come true Gian," Shamala gently intoned. "Sometimes the most expected moments happen to us during unexpected times. And constantly fretting on our wishes and desires will turn our thoughts dark. So it is better to just let it go. What is destined for you will reach you by God's grace.

"Agree. I did what you said twenty five years ago; letting my love to go and living in hope that one day my love would return one day." Gian ended.

There's a deep silence between them.

"Shamala, do you still remember our last meeting after the party at my house?" Gian asked.

Shamala nodded as sign that she still remembers that day.

"You asked me not to go missing, but I didn't expect that you will go missing for 25 years Shamala," Gian smiled bitterly.

"I'm sorry Gian," Shamala apologized. "During that time, the situation was so difficult for me, where suddenly and somehow I have to leave."

"It's okay Shamala. I know you. Just that, I missed you a lot. Whenever I feel down, I would think of you, your positive words, your patience and your smile. And yeah … somehow I survived without …" Gian unable to finish the lines.

Tears could be seen dwelling in Shamala's eyes. Words were finding ways to come out from Shamala but something is stopping her.

I'm finding hard to believe what happened to us — what's still happening to us Gian. I'm really sorry.

"Shamala, I'm sorry." Gian could not withstand seeing his friend crying silently beside him. He felt bad. "Don't cry Shamala. Please… This supposed to be a happy vacation for you, but because of me … Come, let's go around."

From tasting unsalted bread to different tasting of bread, and not forgetting museum of Michael Angelo at Florence, next the guest from Malaysia were brought to Venice. The melodious sound of gondolicrs singing, and the aromatic smell of fresh pastries making their way out, creates a soothing and relaxing environment. Intricate old building can be seen everywhere.

"I could not believe that we are going back home," Kanmani exclaimed vehemently while packing her things up.

"We were enjoying ourselves that much, which is why we did not feel time, had passed," Rhea continued. "We certainly will miss this place. Uncle Gian, we will miss you too. Thank you so much uncle for the great hostage and tour. We feel contented.

Gian smiled, "It is the least that I can do for you all. I'm sorry if I had lacked somewhere."

"Oh! No uncle. No sorry please," Kanmani interrupted. "We are the one who supposed to ask sorry if we had troubled you."

"Not at all ladies. I extremely enjoyed all the moments with you," Gian replied. "Shall we move? It's better to be early to the airport."

"Sure. Let me get the luggage. And where is *periamma*?" Rhea looking for Shamala.

"I know where she would be. You all get ready and I'll bring her. Don't forget your passports," Gian reminded.

Gian wheeled to his praying area and spotted Shamala lighting some candles. He waited for her to finish her prayers.

"I knew what you pray to Jesus?" Gian started when Shamala turned after finishing her prayers.

Shamala smiled. "I don't know that my friend is good in mind reading."

Gian grinned hearing that words from Shamala. "Come let's go. They are waiting outside."

Shamala paused for a moment. She strolled towards Gian and slowly she kneeled down in front of Gian, looking straight into his eyes. "Take a good care of yourself. Remember you are not young anymore. Don't forget your medicine and stop worrying. Okay?"

"Done," Gian questioned sarcastically. "I've been doing this all the time."

"Oooo okay. Then take care," Shamala stood up, patted Gian's back as signaling that she is leaving. That is when, Gian pulled Shamala hand which makes her stop from getting away from Gian. Her heart starts to beat fast. Slowly she turned to see Gian. His eyes are already full with tears.

"Don't go Shamala," sobbed Gian.

Shamala felt so weak. She felt so heavy that made her to kneel down again. The moment that she tried to avoid all this while, but somehow it appears in her life. "Time had passed Gian. I don't find this right. We are not young anymore."

"But our love is. Our love is still young. You can't deny that sweetheart," Gian bringing Shamala's hand close to his heart. "I need you Shamala. Please don't go."

Shamala did not say a word. She tried to loosen her hand from Gian's grip. "I need to go."

Shamala went away from Gian, wiping her tears off. Getting all her bags from the room that she stayed, Shamala walked to the living room. Everyone is ready with their bags and the figure which she left at the room was also present there.

"Shall we move *periamma*?" Rhea asked.

Shamala nodded and straight away scooted towards the door. She bent down to pick her ankle boots from the shelf, but she couldn't. Her hand trembles as she was battling with something which she couldn't identify, something which she feels wrong and something which is stopping her from moving forward. In the end she gave up. Shamala was defeated by the 'something' her own emotions. She turned to find for the one who brought her to that state and spotted a silent smile on that person. She started to weep.

Noticing this, Rhea, Kanmani and Kaaviya went puzzled looking at both Shamala and Gian. One was smiling and another one was crying.

Gian wheeled towards Shamala and grabbed her hand. "What is destined for me, finally it had reached me by God's grace," Gian repeating the lines said by Shamala at the Trevi Fountain. "I love you Shamala, please don't go away."

With tears flowing continuously, there was a soft light in Shamala eyes as she looked at Gian. "This time I won't Gian," and she kneeled down to hug him.

"One ticket need to be canceled then," Rhea chuckled accompanied with laughter from Kaaviya and Kanmani.

LOVE. The only emotion which makes the blind to see, the deaf to hear, the mute to speak, the abnormal to be normal and the normal to be abnormal. Don't get me started about love and affection. For it's a long story —*The Village Princess.*

-The End-

Rampria Mohana Sundaram is a high school graduate from SMK. Taman Desa Skudai and one of the top student in Sijil Pelajaran Malaysia (SPM). She is also known as a Sapphire figure for English language in her school. Being an author for this book creates a strong landmark for her future profession in filming industry.

Printed in the United States
By Bookmasters